PICTURE WINDOW BOOKS
a capstone imprint

One of the greatest heroes of Greek mythology was Jason. Promised the king's throne if he could deliver the Golden Fleece, Jason set out on a quest.

The sorceress Medea helped Jason overcome many deadly challenges. She did these things because she wanted power and riches. She wanted to be Jason's queen when he claimed the throne of Iolcus. But when Jason and Medea returned to Iolcus with the Golden Fleece, King Pelias refused to step down. Medea used her dark magic to trick the king's daughters into cutting Pelias into pieces. But instead of making Jason the king, the angry people of Iolcus drove Jason and Medea out of the city forever.

That's the classic version of the story.

But how would Medea tell it?

I am Medea—just Medea.

If you have read other stories about me, you might think my name is "The Sorceress Medea." Or "Medea the Witch." Or "Medea, Who Practiced Dark Magic."

The stories tell of cruel things I did for selfish reasons. But the truth is, magic was done TO ME! The goddess Hera *used* me to settle a grudge. And when the gods get involved, you don't have much choice about how you act.

Here's the real story.

3

Before Jason and his Argonauts arrived in my father's land, I was happy. My dad was the king of Colchis, and I had many privileges. I didn't think about love or power.

But Jason changed all that.

A little history: Jason's uncle, King Pelias, had taken the throne of Iolcus from Jason's dad. Pelias promised Jason he would give it back if Jason brought him the Golden Fleece. The Golden Fleece lay far away, across dangerous seas—right in the heart of Colchis. A dragon protected it day and night.

Pelias knew getting the Golden Fleece would be nearly impossible. He didn't expect Jason to return.

Jason was strong, brave, and heroic. But he had something else on his side: an angry goddess. It seems that Pelias did not honor Hera, Zeus' wife.

Bad idea.

To get revenge on Pelias, Hera helped Jason on his quest for the Golden Fleece. She helped him build a ship, the *Argo*. She helped him meet challenges along the way to Colchis. And when he got there, she helped him again. And her help involved me.

The first time I met Jason, I thought he was incredibly rude. He wanted that fleece, he said, and he wasn't going to take no for an answer.

"I will give you the Golden Fleece," my father said, "if you earn it." He pointed to the courtyard, where two great bulls kicked and bucked, flames leaping from their mouths. "You must harness those bulls and attach a plow to them. Then you must plow the yard and sow these dragon teeth like seeds."

Jason agreed to the challenge. I knew he wouldn't last two seconds with those bulls. Good riddance, I thought.

I didn't see Aphrodite casting her love spell upon me, or Hera whispering in her ear.

8

Then the spell took hold. BOOM! A feeling like soft lightning filled my heart. One minute, I thought Jason was an arrogant fool. The next, I would have done anything for him.

I told Jason to meet me by the river later that night.

If my father had known, he would have killed me. That's how powerful Aphrodite's spell was. Love blinded me to danger.

"Rub this potion on your body," I told Jason. "It will protect you from the bulls' flames. But beware: When you sow the dragon teeth, armed soldiers will spring from the earth. Throw stones at them. They will become confused and attack each other instead of you."

"What can I give you in return?" Jason asked.

"Take me as your wife," I heard myself say.

He agreed.

The next day, everyone in Colchis came out to watch Jason die fighting the bulls. Jason rubbed the magical potion on his body. He filled a bag with stones. Then he walked out into the courtyard.

When the bulls breathed their fire, the flames didn't hurt Jason at all. Everyone cheered—everyone except my father, that is.

Jason got the harness on the bulls and marched them around the courtyard, plowing the dirt.

My father fumed.

When Jason finished sowing the dragon teeth, the crowd cheered even louder. And when the soldiers burst from the earth, Jason hurled the stones at them. Confused, they attacked each other instead of Jason, and the fight was over quickly.

"I have done what you asked," Jason said.
"The Golden Fleece is mine now."

My father was stunned. He had been certain Jason
would not survive the challenge. "Never!" he cried.

I took Jason aside and whispered, "Meet me by the Golden Fleece. Hurry!"

The Golden Fleece hung in a tree nearby, guarded by a huge dragon.

"I cannot defeat that dragon!" Jason said.

"Leave that to me," I said with a wink.

I began to chant. My words stirred magic in the air, and the dragon's great wings dropped. Its massive talons relaxed. Then it set its head on the dirt and fell asleep.

"Amazing," Jason said.

My heart nearly burst with love and pride.

Jason scrambled on top of the sleeping dragon. He snatched the fleece, and the two of us dashed to his ship.

A call rang out in Colchis. "After them!" Father sent troops to kill us.

Do you see how blinded I was by Aphrodite's love spell? I made my father so angry he wished to KILL ME. But I didn't care! All I wanted to do was help Jason.

The *Argo* escaped my father's navy and sailed safely back to Iolcus. The moment was finally here. Jason would take the throne, and I would become queen.

King Pelias took one look at Jason and the Golden Fleece and turned pale. He couldn't believe Jason had done it.

"I am king now!" Jason declared.

"Never!" Pelias shouted. "Take him away!"

The guards seized Jason and forced him from the city.

I was heartbroken.

As for what happened next ... well, I still can't believe I did it. Love makes you do crazy, crazy things.

I told the king's daughters about a magic potion I had that would make their father young again. But there was a trick to it. First they would have to chop their dad into pieces. I showed them how the potion worked on a chopped-up ram. I poured the potion over the pieces, and the animal came together again, young and healthy.

But when the daughters chopped up their father, I didn't give them the potion. They had no way to bring the king back to life.

I thought for sure my beloved would take the throne after that. Pelias was dead, and Jason was the rightful heir. Instead, my trick filled the people of Iolcus with rage. They kicked us out of the city. And the worst of it?

Jason left me to marry someone else.

It's terrible what I did to Pelias. I know. But believe me, I wasn't thinking like myself. I'm not a monster. I didn't want things to happen the way they did.

But Hera did. She got her revenge on Pelias, and she used *me* to do it.

Hmm ... I wonder if she could help me get Jason back.

Critical Thinking Using the Common Core

This version of the classic Greek myth "Jason and the Golden Fleece" is told by Medea, from her point of view. If Jason told the story, what details might he tell differently? What if Medea's father told the story from his point of view? (Integration of Knowledge and Ideas)

Medea claims that the goddess Hera used her to get revenge on King Pelias. She says she wouldn't have helped Jason if she hadn't been under a spell. Do you believe her? Why or why not? Give examples to support your answer. (Integration of Knowledge and Ideas)

Jason goes on a long, difficult journey to get the Golden Fleece and return it to King Pelias. He must clear many hurdles. Describe Jason's challenges in the order in which they happened. Then explain how Hera and Medea helped Jason overcome the challenges. (Craft and Structure)

Glossary

Argonaut—one of Jason's men who sailed with him on the ship *Argo*

Golden Fleece—the golden coat of a magical ram

heir—someone who has been or will be left a title, property, or money

Iolcus (ee-OHL-kus)—a city in Ancient Greece, and home to Jason

mythology—old or ancient stories told again and again that help connect people with their past

point of view—a way of looking at something

sorceress—a woman who controls evil spirits to perform magic

sow—to scatter seeds over the ground so they will grow

version—an account of something from a certain point of view

Read More

Gunderson, Jessica. *Jason and the Argonauts: A Retelling.* Mankato, Minn.: Picture Window Books, 2012.

Jeffrey, Gary. *Jason and the Argonauts.* Graphic Mythical Heroes. New York: Gareth Stevens Pub., 2013.

Whitehead, Dan. *Jason and the Argonauts.* Mythology. New Delhi: Campfire, 2011.

Yomtov, Nel, retold by. *Jason and the Golden Fleece.* Graphic Revolve. Minneapolis: Stone Arch Books, 2009.

Internet Sites

FactHound offers a safe, fun way to find Internet sites related to this book. All of the sites on FactHound have been researched by our staff.

Here's all you do:

Visit *www.facthound.com*

Type in this code: 9781479521838

Check out projects, games and lots more at
www.capstonekids.com

Thanks to our advisers for their expertise, research, and advice:

Susan C. Shelmerdine, PhD, Professor of Classical Studies
University of North Carolina, Greensboro

Terry Flaherty, PhD, Professor of English
Minnesota State University, Mankato

Editor: Jill Kalz
Designer: Lori Bye
Art Director: Nathan Gassman
Production Specialist: Danielle Ceminsky
The illustrations in this book were created digitally.

Picture Window Books are published by Capstone,
1710 Roe Crest Drive, North Mankato, Minnesota 56003
www.capstonepub.com

Library of Congress Cataloging-in-Publication Data
Braun, Eric, 1971–
  Medea tells all : a mad, magical love / by Eric Braun; illustrated by Stephen Gilpin.
    pages cm.—(Nonfiction picture books. The other side of the myth.)
  Summary: "Introduces the concept of point of view through Medea's retelling of the
classic Greek myth 'Jason and the Golden Fleece'"—Provided by publisher.
  ISBN 978-1-4795-2183-8 (library binding)
  ISBN 978-1-4795-2958-2 (paper over board)
  ISBN 978-1-4795-2940-7 (paperback)
  ISBN 978-1-4795-3319-0 (eBook PDF)
1. Medea (Greek mythology)—Juvenile literature. I. Gilpin, Stephen, illustrator. II. Title.
BL820.M37B73 2014
398.20938'02—dc23   2013032210

About the Author

Eric Braun has written and edited hundreds of books for readers of all ages. He blames the bad ones on Hera. Eric lives in Minneapolis with his wife and sons. Go to heyericbraun.com to learn more.

Look for all the books in the series:

CYCLOPS TELLS ALL: THE WAY EYE SEE IT
MEDEA TELLS ALL: A MAD, MAGICAL LOVE
MEDUSA TELLS ALL: BEAUTY MISSING, HAIR HISSING
PANDORA TELLS ALL: NOT THE CURIOUS KIND

Printed in the United States of America in Brainerd, Minnesota.
092013   007770BANGS14